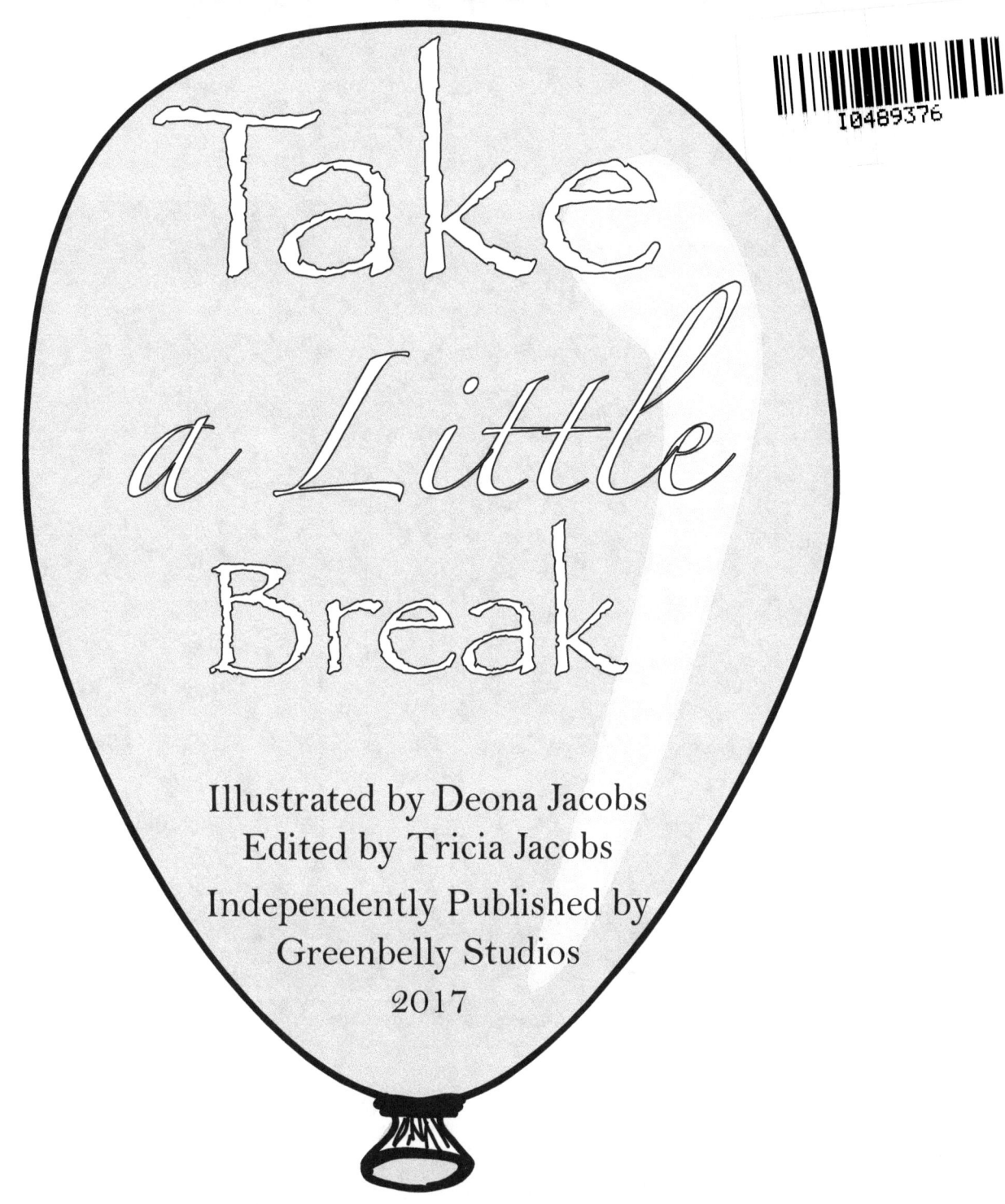

Take a Little Break

Illustrated by Deona Jacobs

Edited by Tricia Jacobs

Independently Published by
Greenbelly Studios

2017

Ordering Information:
Quantity sales. Special discounts are available on quantity purchases by corporations, associations, and others. For details, contact the publisher at the website address below.
Please contact Greenbelly Studios www.greenbelly.biz with any questions, comments, or suggestions.

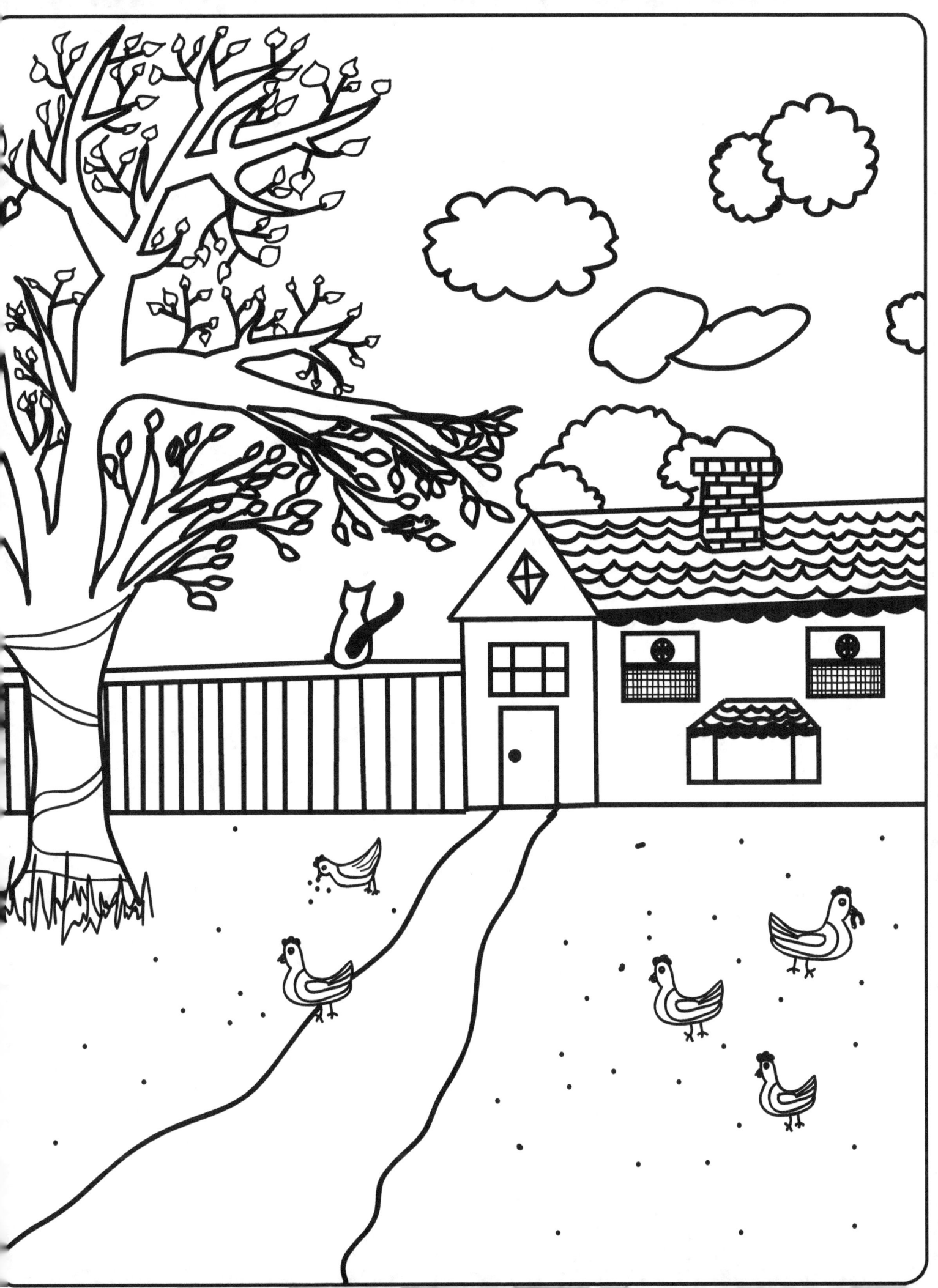

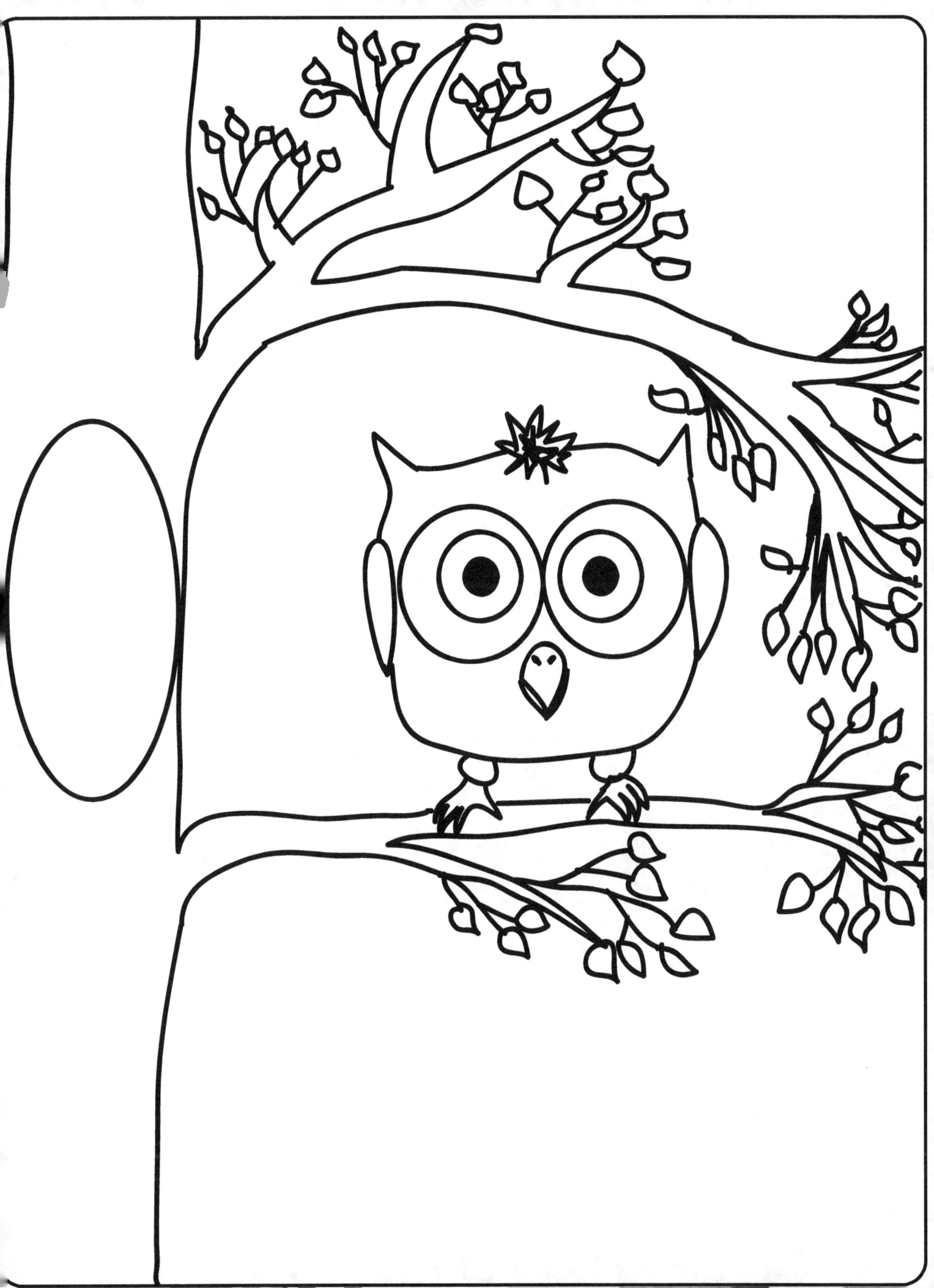

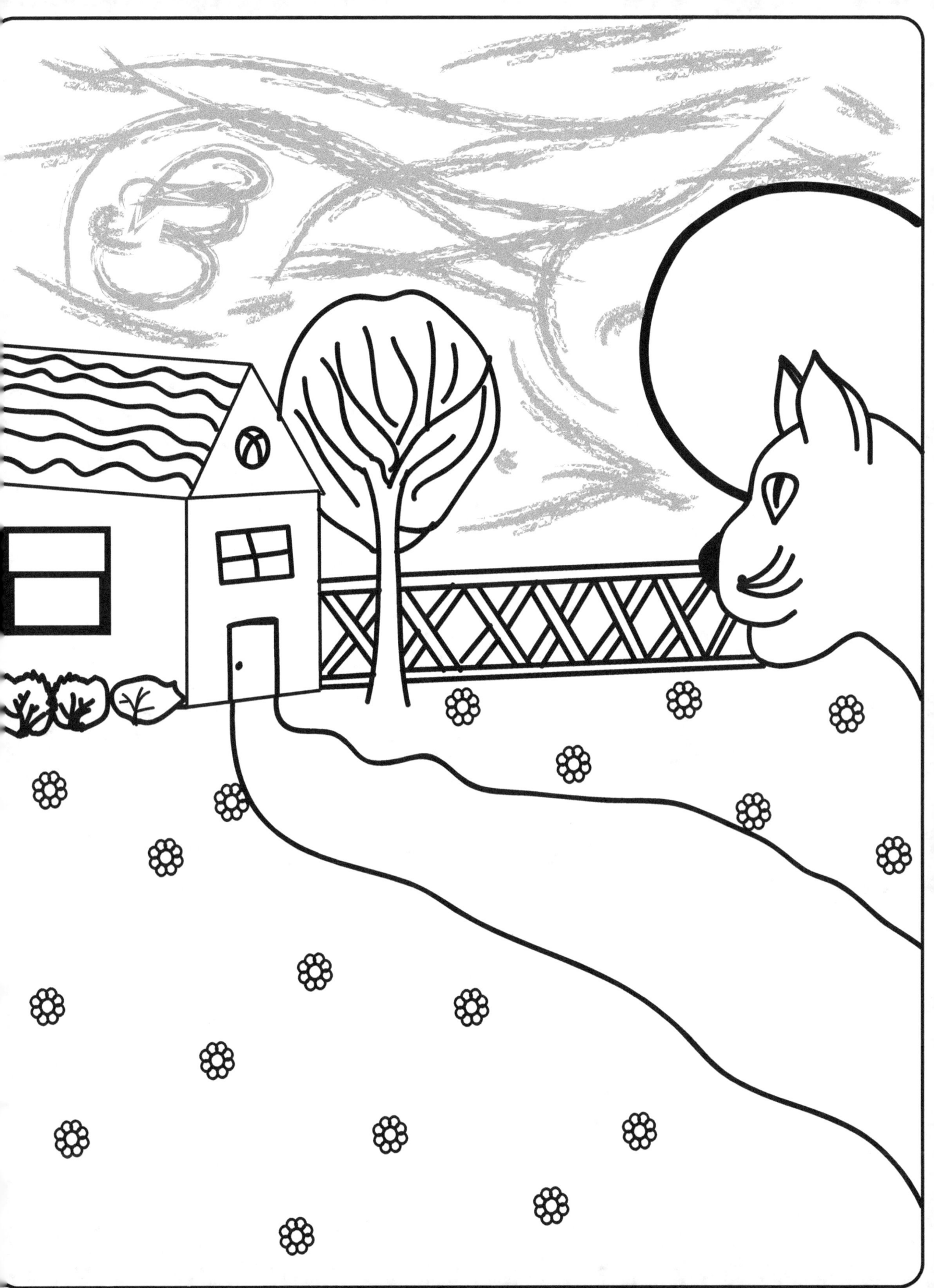

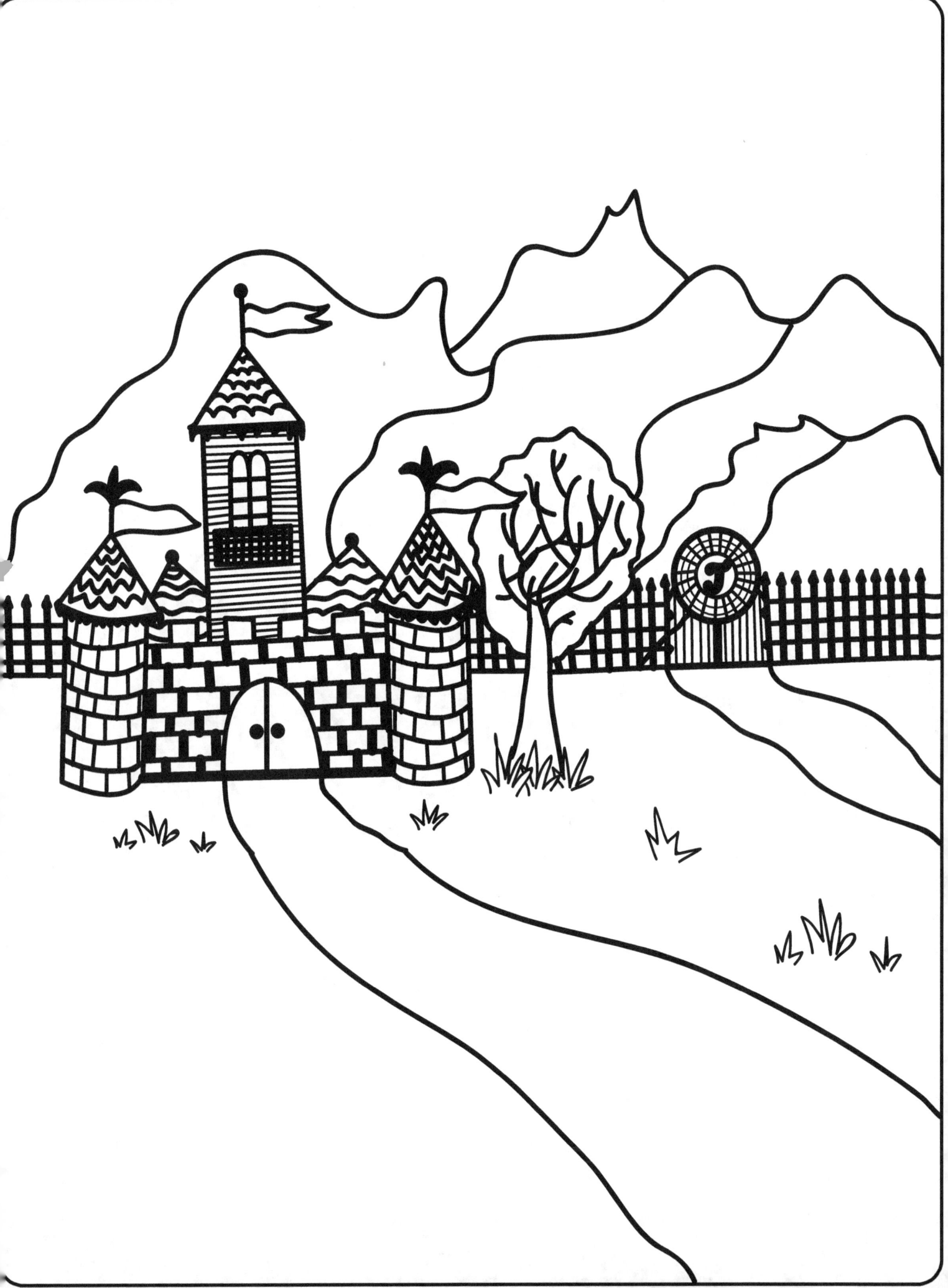

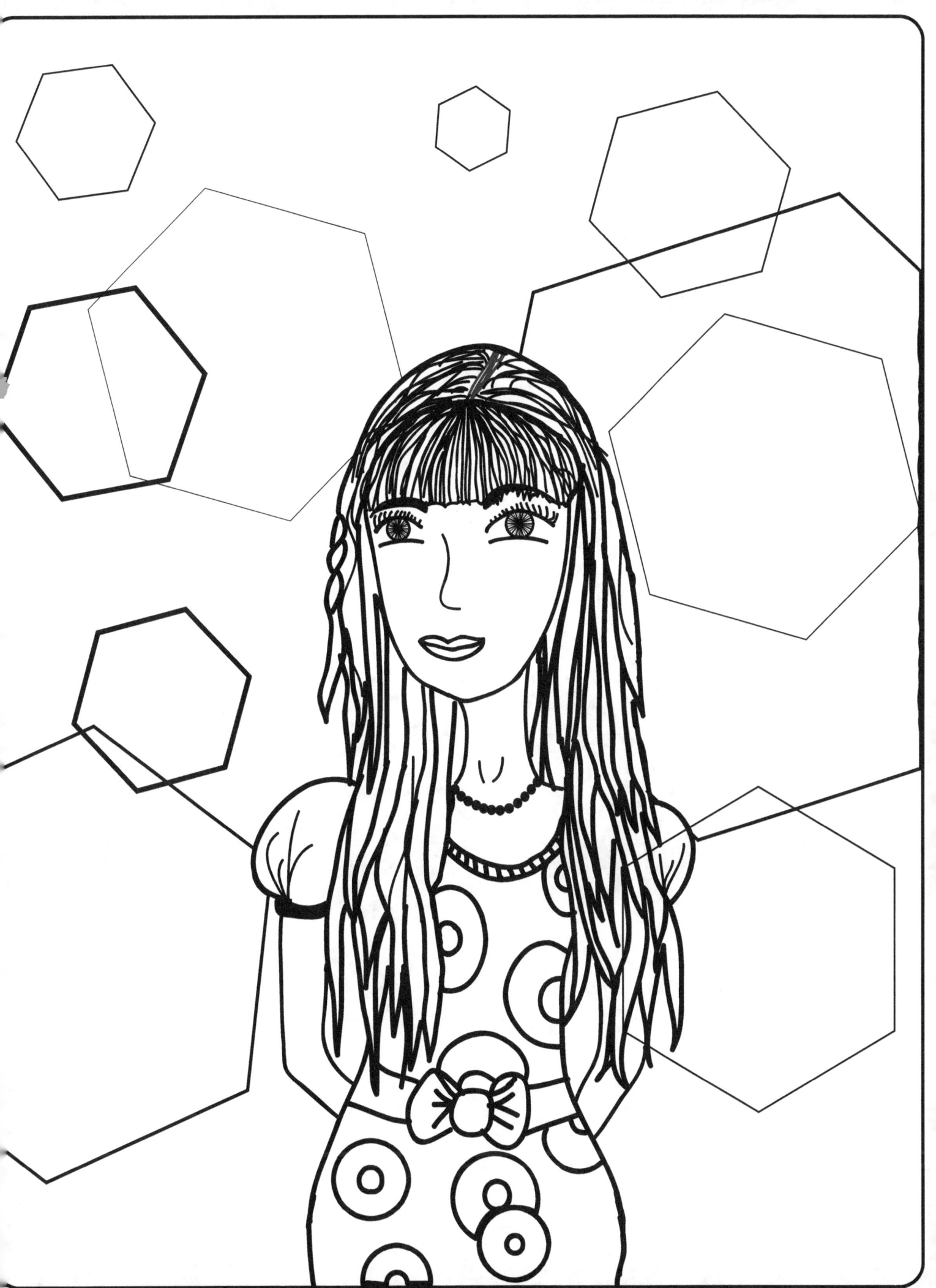

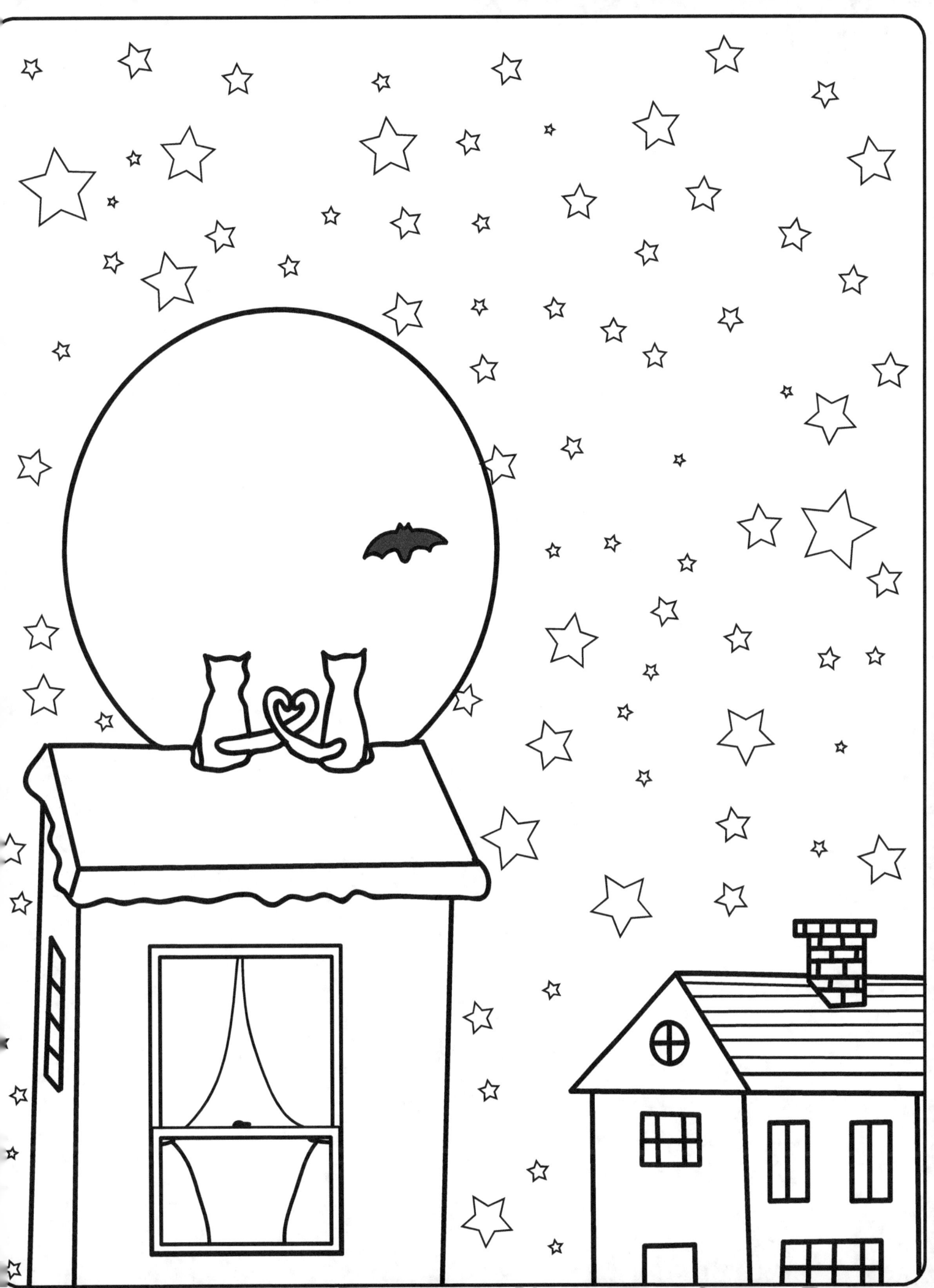

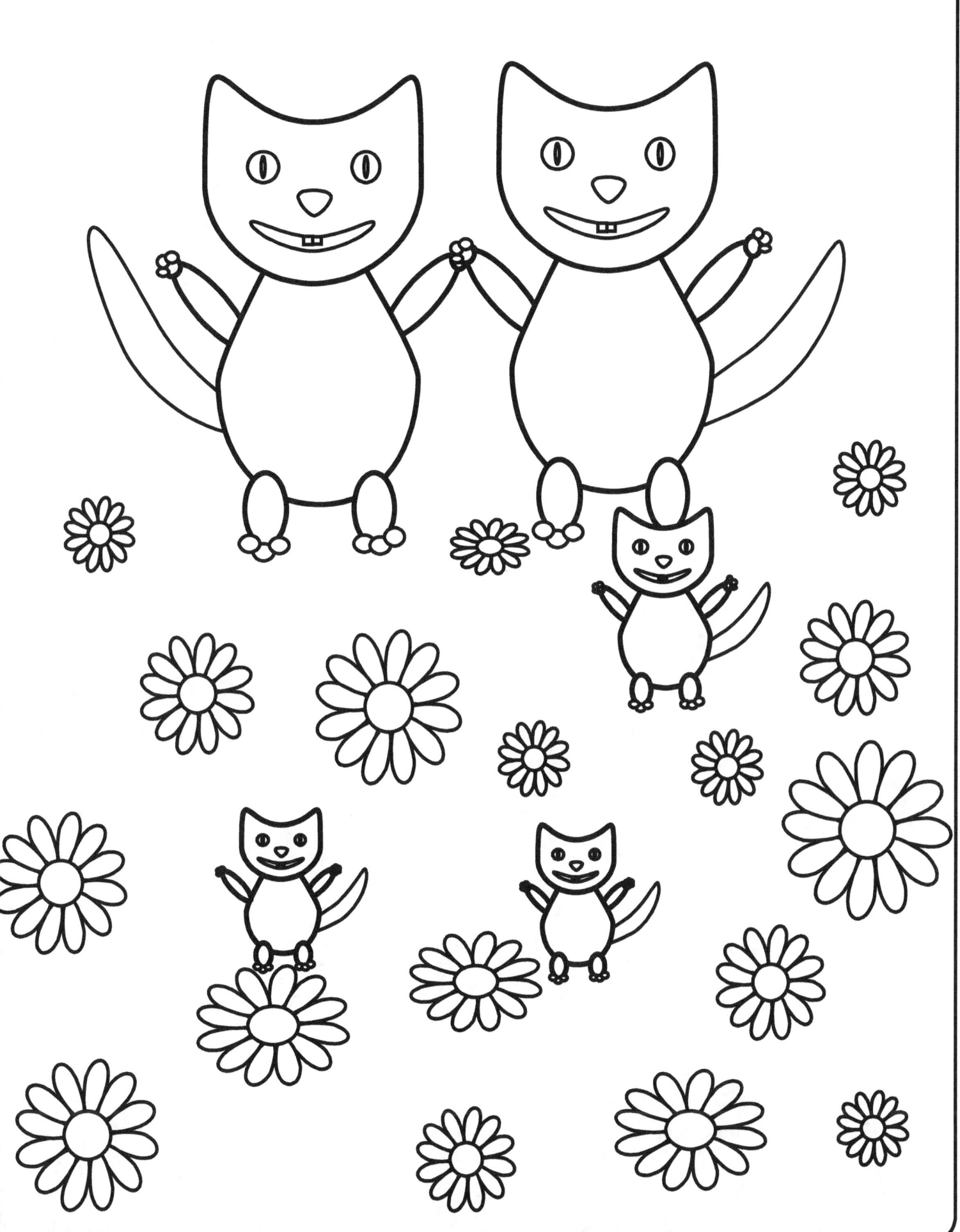

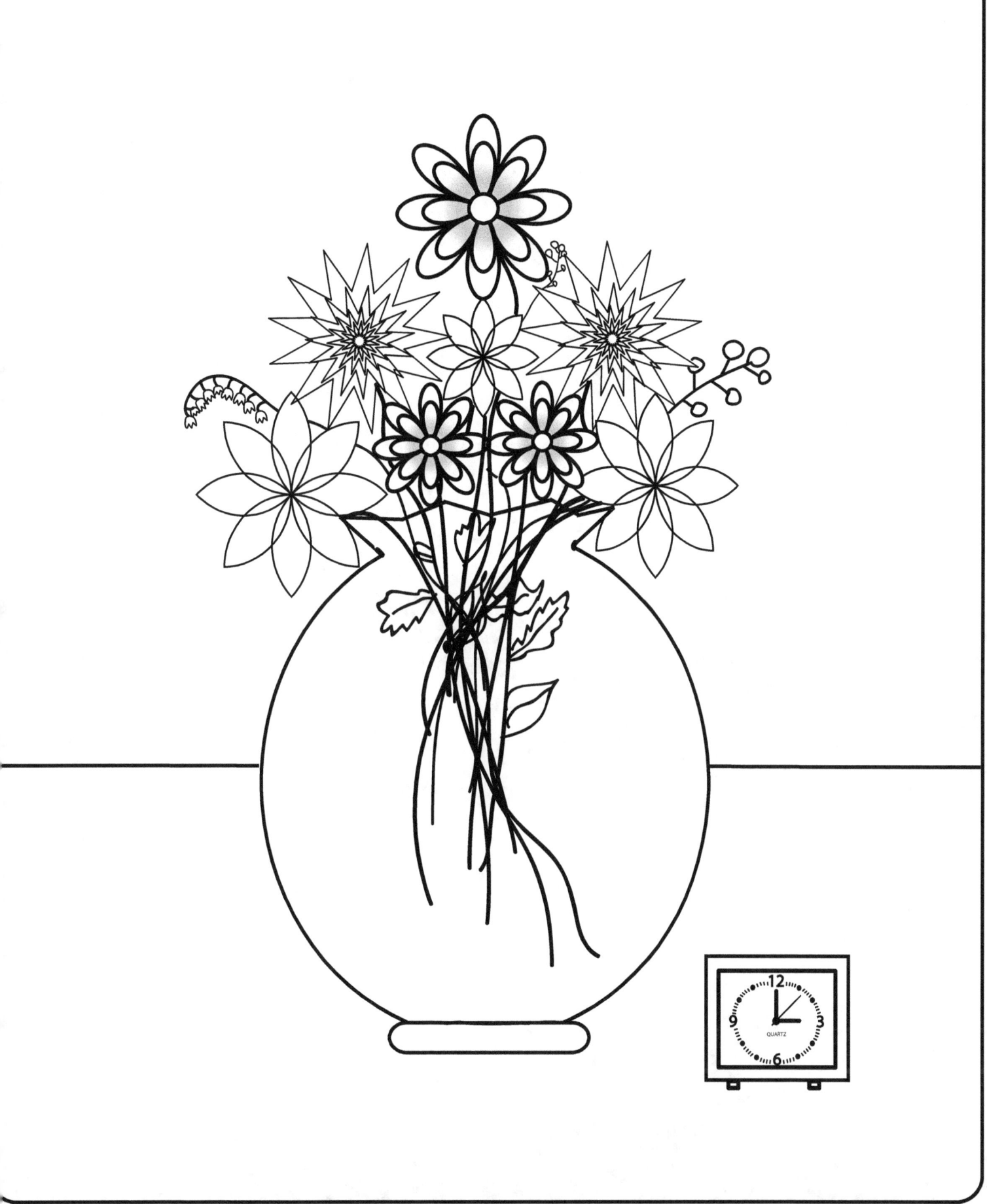

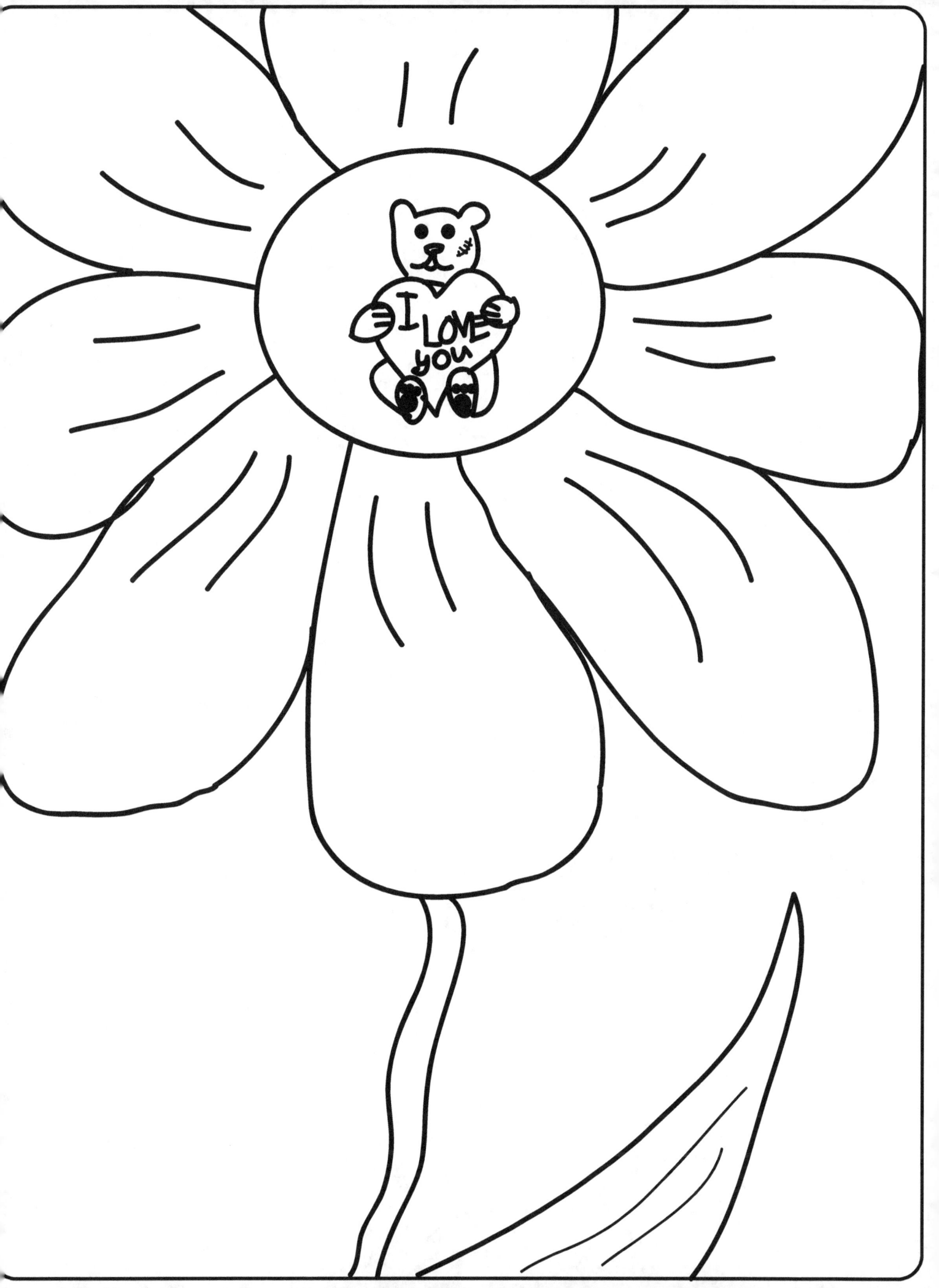

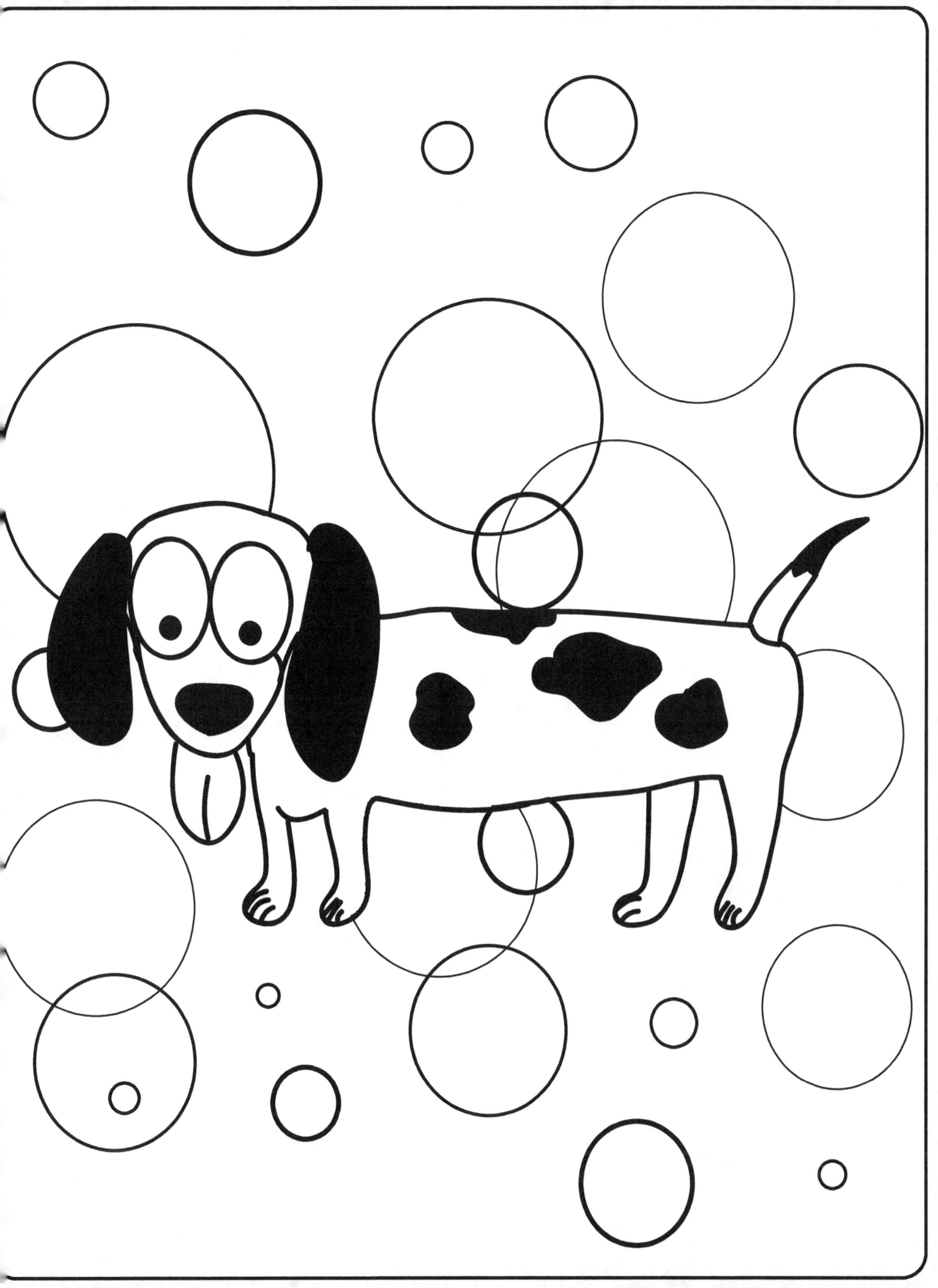

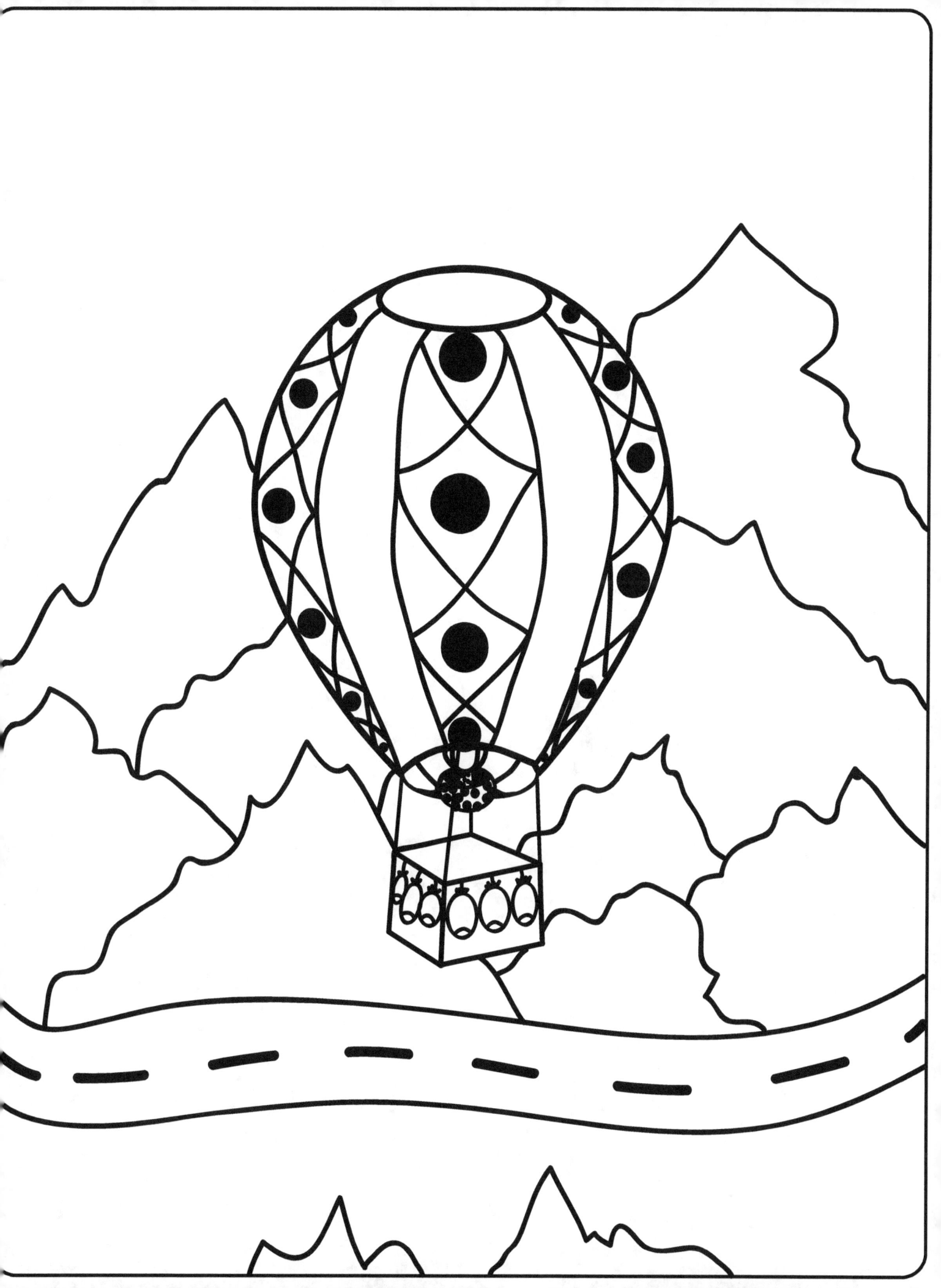

Doodles

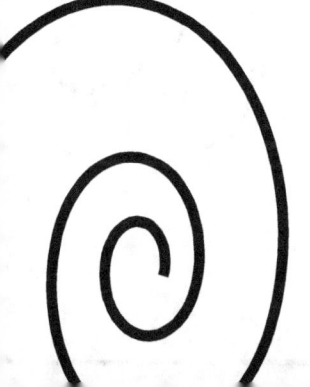

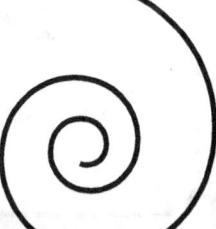

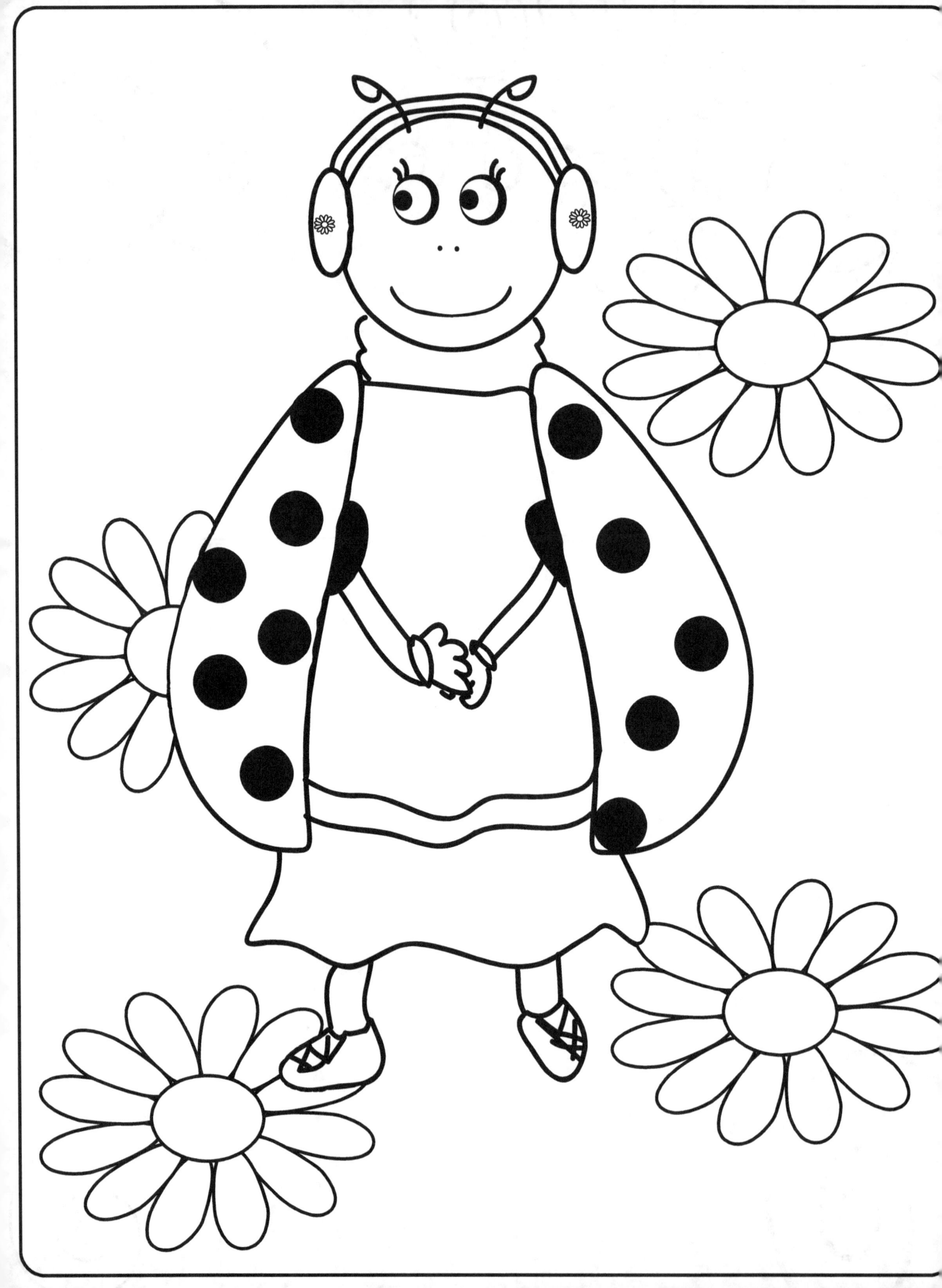

Doodles

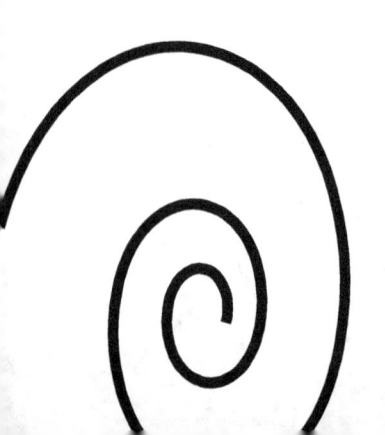
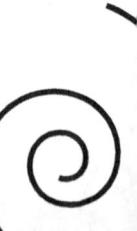

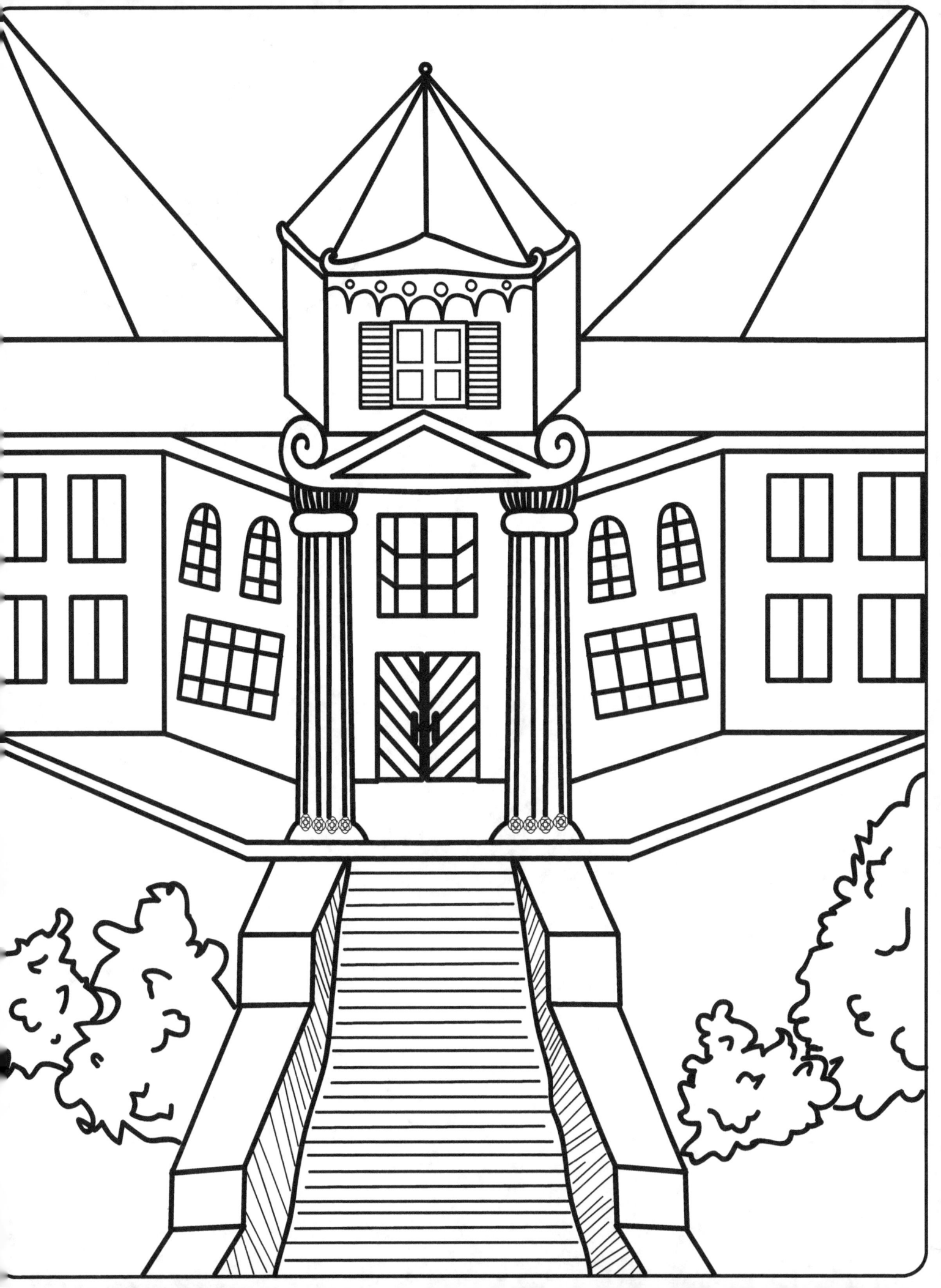

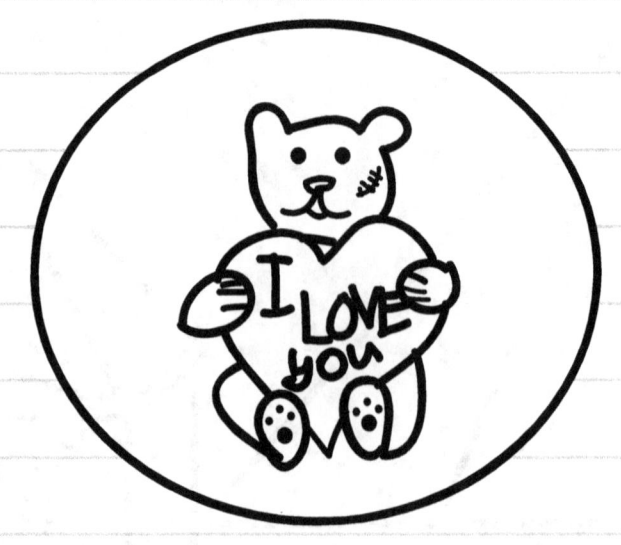

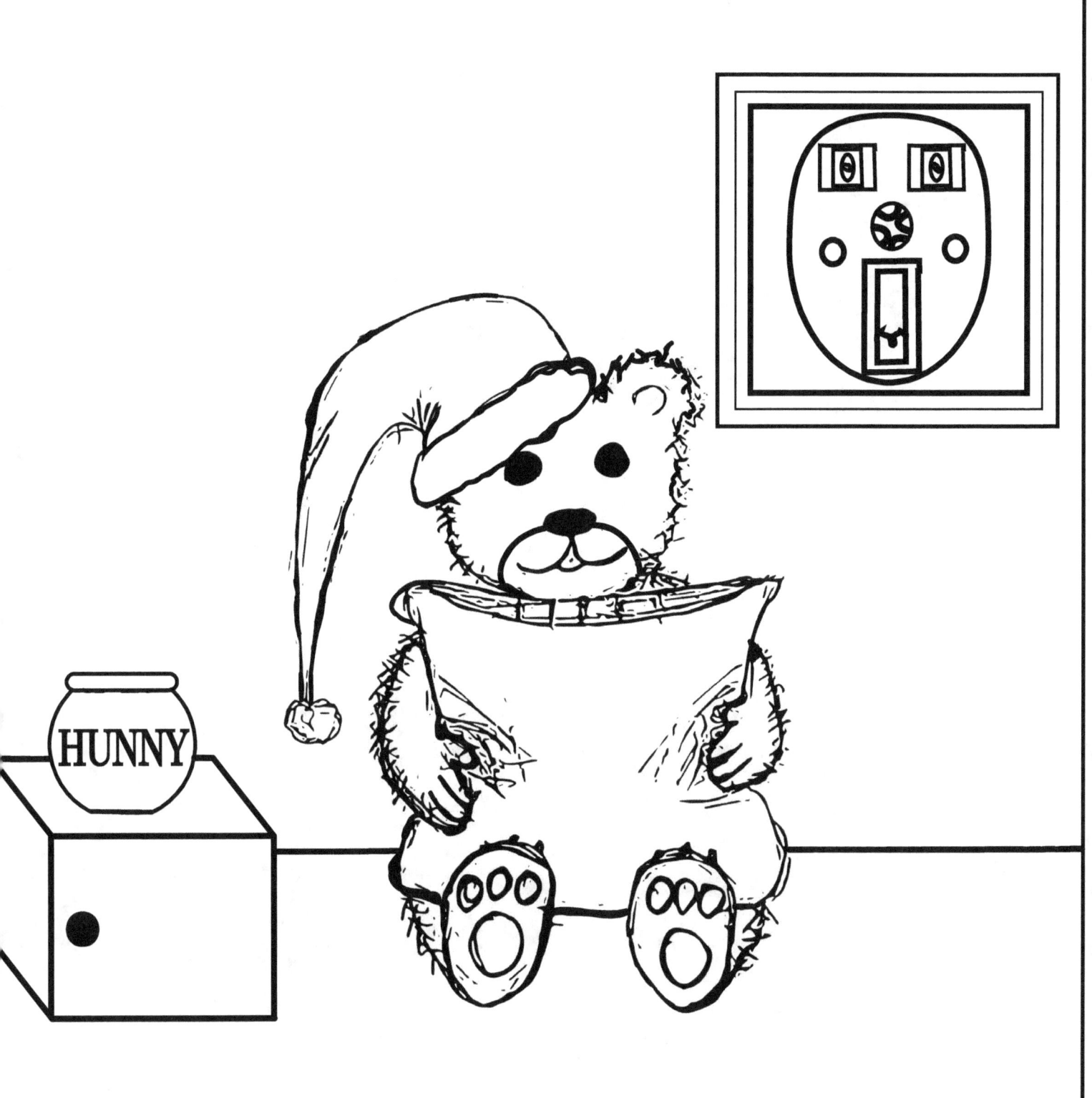

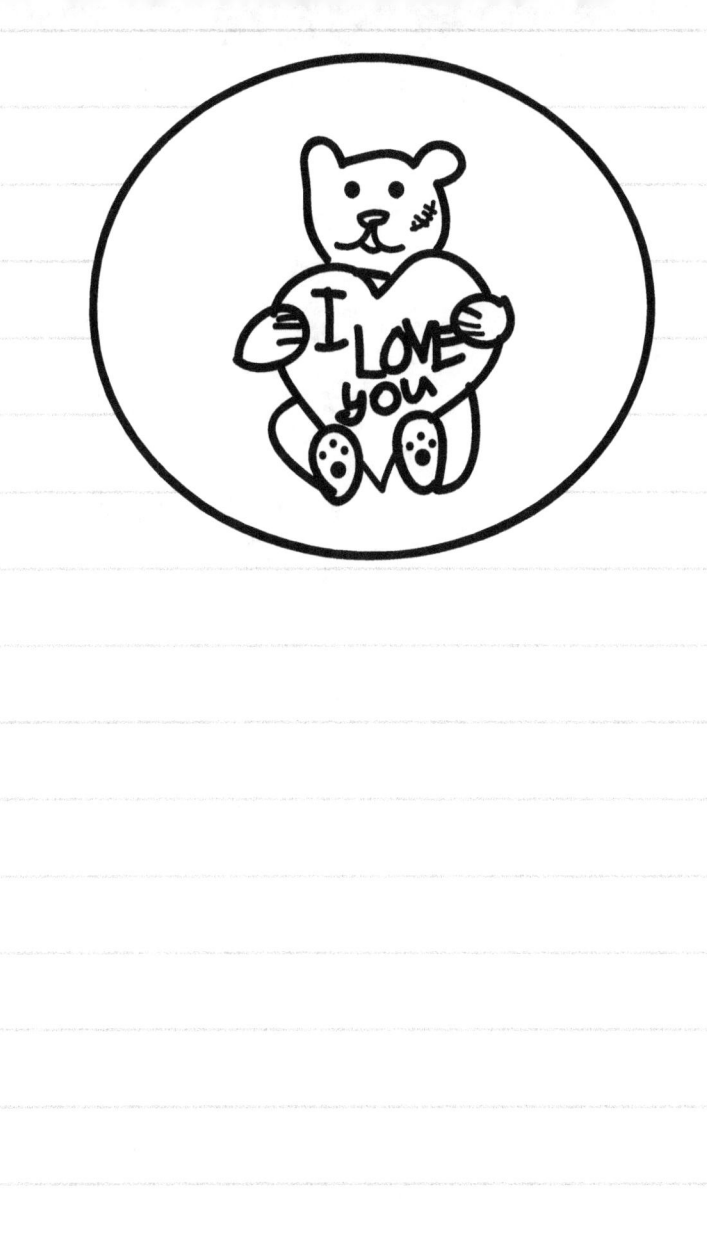

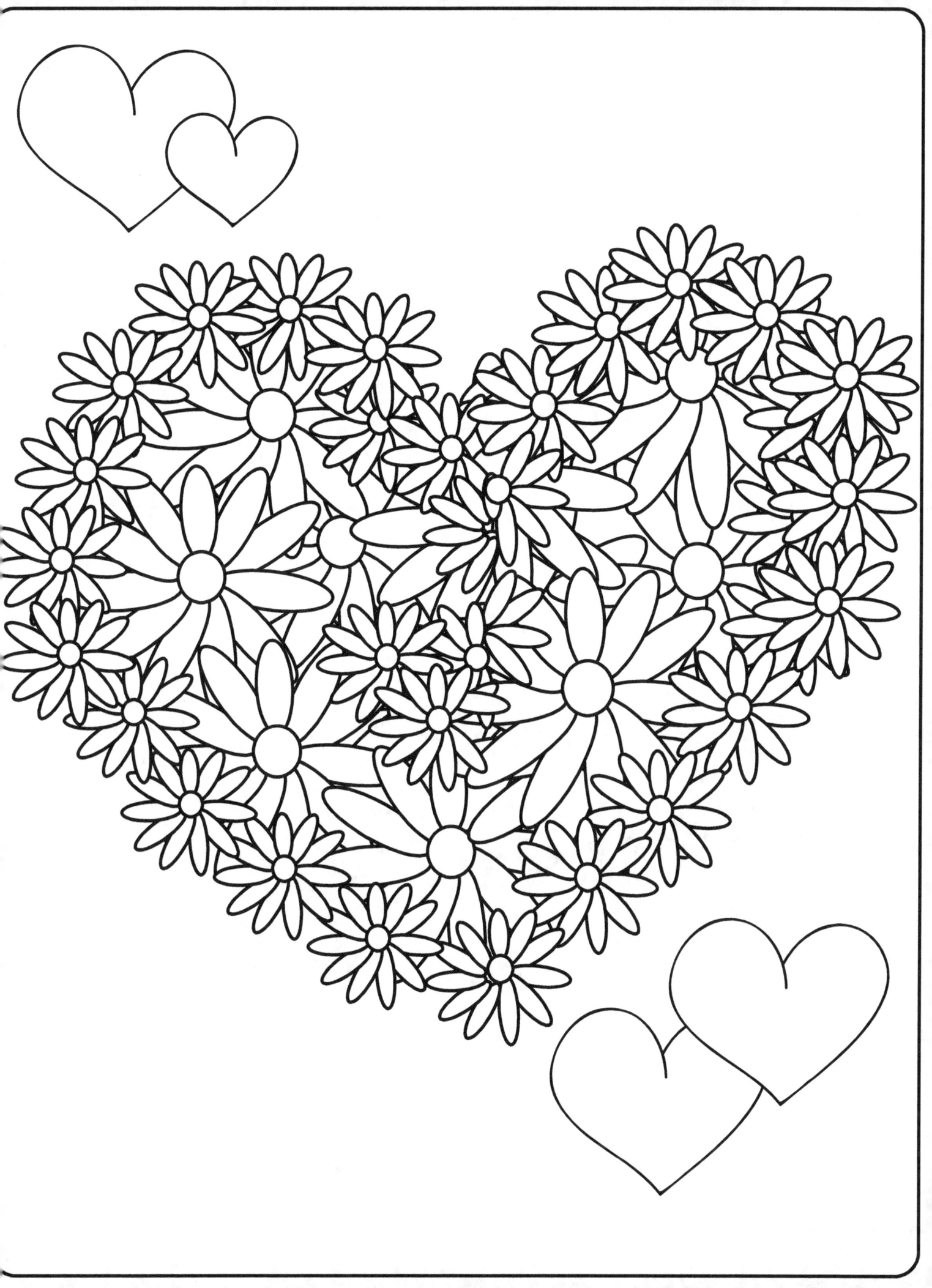

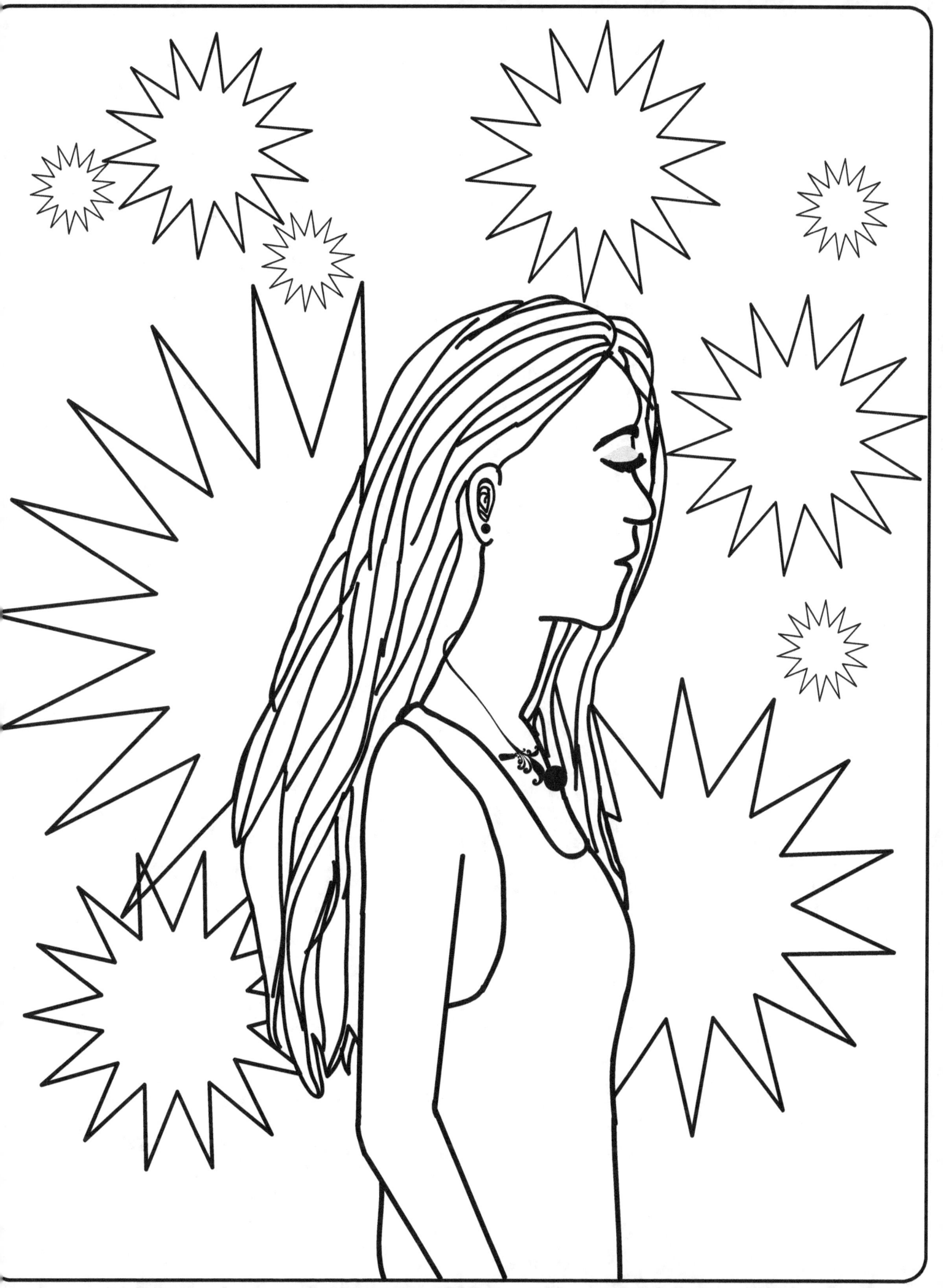

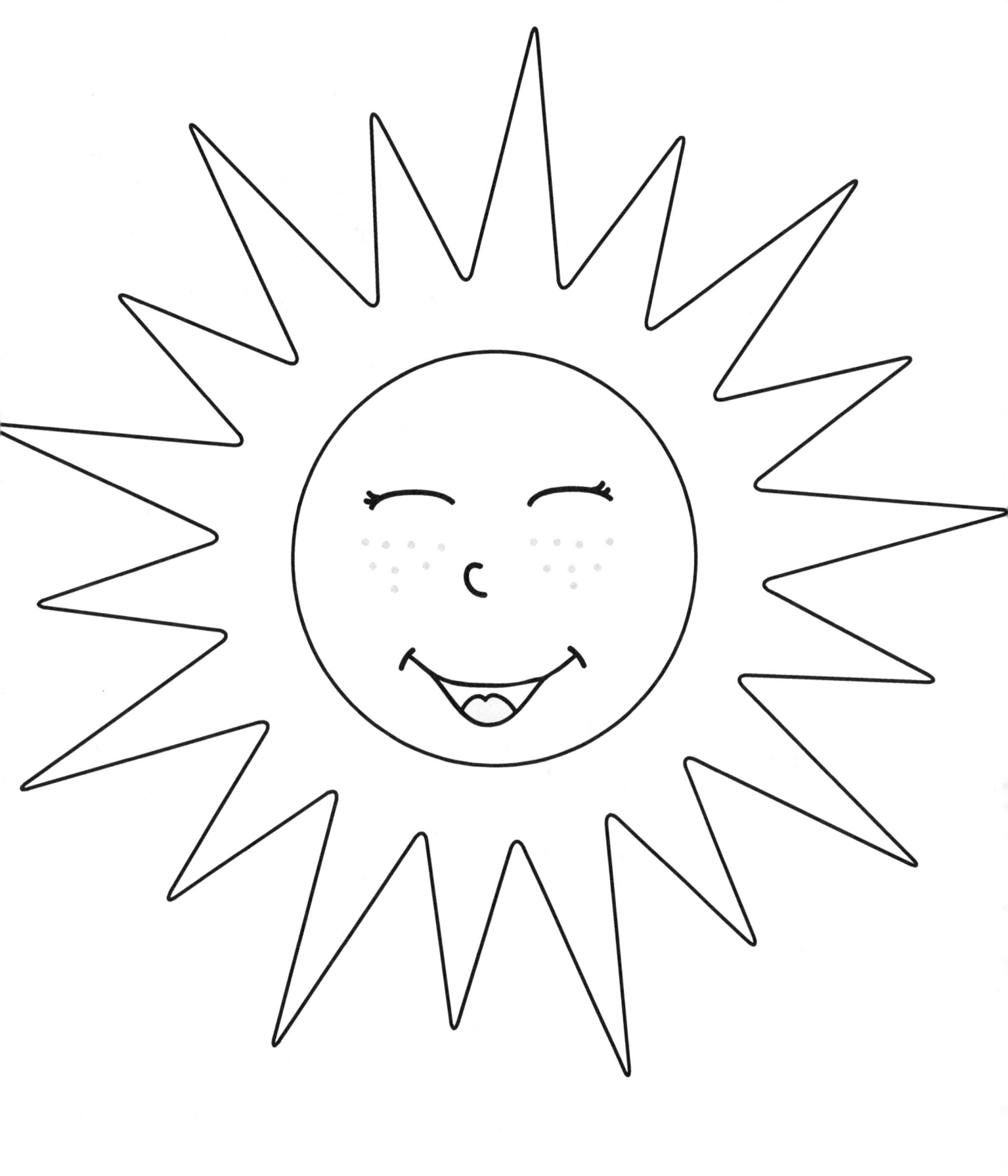

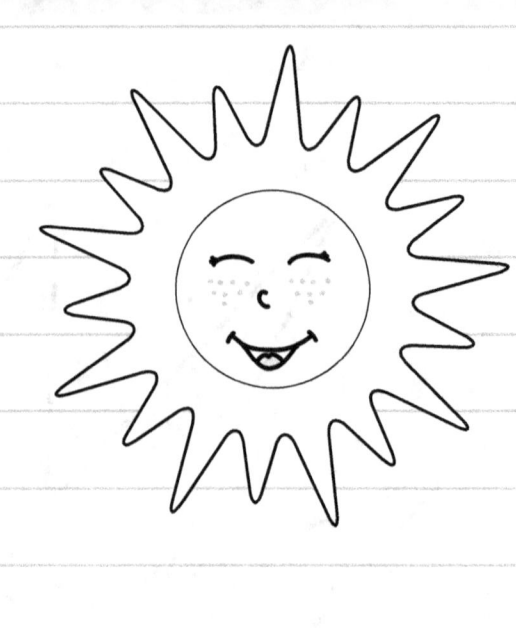